Sex
on the Net

**The dilemma
of policing
cyberspace**

Yaman Akdeniz

Sex on the Net
The dilemma of policing cyberspace

South Street Press is an imprint of
Garnet Publishing Limited

Published by
Garnet Publishing Limited
8 Southern Court
South Street
Reading
RG1 4QS
UK

ISBN 1 902932 00 5

First Edition 1999

British Library Cataloguing-in-Publication
Data. A catalogue record for this book is
available from the British Library.

House editor: Natalie Hutchin
Jacket and book design: Michael Hinks
Printed in Lebanon

Contents

Introduction

Pornography is not new. Since the invention of the printing press, pornography and sexually explicit publications have been circulating in one form or another, typically underground. The Marquis de Sade's *120 Days of Sodom* is one of the most famous examples of literature with a sexually explicit content, and it wasn't published until after the French Revolution. Until the 1990s pornography was available mainly in the format of magazines, books and videos, but now the whole industry has been revolutionised following the development and widespread availability of the Internet. Sexually explicit material on the Internet extends from the modestly titillating to the hardest-core.

One thing is clear in relation to pornography: it means big business. The American porn industry, one of the biggest, earns an estimated $8 to $10 billion a year and this includes trade through the Internet. The porn industry has in many ways been a pioneer of the development of electronic commerce, a leading force in the commercialisation of the Internet. It offers, in return for payment through the World Wide Web (WWW), photographs, erotic text and audio stories, video clips including live feeds, live sex chat, and almost any format or scenario imaginable from straight sex to gay and lesbian to fetish and ultra hard-core sexual encounters, side by side with specialised themes such as Asian babes and celebrity porn.

Of course, political debate about whether pornography is harmful to women and whether it should be censored is almost as old as the industry itself. How pornography should be regulated has been one of the most controversial topics to have arisen in relation to the Internet in recent years. Its widespread availability has stirred up a moral panic shared by many governments, law enforcement bodies, prosecutors and judges, along with the media in general. Although sex on the Net has been freely available for a long time, regulatory initiatives within the USA in 1996 mean that things are already changing. Since early 1996, for instance, the US porn industry has been operating with password-protected schemes in which the users have to provide their credit card numbers (and their credit) in order to access pornographic content.

However, one of the problems preventing governments from taking an effective legislative hold on the industry is that there is no settled definition of pornography, either in the United Kingdom itself or within a global environment such as the Internet, where cultural, moral and legal variations all around the world make it difficult to define 'pornographic content' in a way acceptable to all. The Williams Committee on Obscenity and Film Censorship, set up to review all obscenity laws, attempted to define pornography in the following terms in 1979:

> We take it that, as almost everyone understands the term, a pornographic representation is one that combines two features: it has a certain function or intention, to arouse its audience sexually, and also a certain content, explicit representations of sexual material (organs, postures, activity, etc.). A work has to have both this function and this content to be a piece of pornography.

But what is considered simply pornographic but not obscene in the UK may well be obscene in many other countries; conversely, what is considered lawful and pornographic in, for example, Sweden may well be obscene under current UK legislation. Despite obscenity being a concept recognised by law, there is no global legal definition for pornography.

From the 1960s to the 1990s the range and content of pornography have changed dramatically. The existing legislation, such as the UK Obscene Publications Act 1959 and 1964, was introduced to deal with literature and photographs. Now pornography is available in different formats, including video tapes, CD-ROMs and online. There have been many attempts to limit the availability of pornographic content on the Internet by governments and law enforcement bodies all around the world. The US government introduced its Communications Decency Act in 1996, and the UK police attempted to censor Usenet discussion groups allegedly carrying child pornography in the summer of 1996. Issues that have arisen in the US and UK in this respect will be dealt with in greater depth later in this guide.

Child pornography is arguably not really a form of pornography at all, and in many countries its production, possession and distribution is illegal as in most cases it involves some form of child abuse. Most of the policing activity over the Internet revolves around the availability of child pornography and its circulation by paedophiles. Later sections will explore police response to child pornography on a global scale covering issues of illegality and will show that the problems connected with child pornography can be different from those surrounding other sexually explicit adult pornography, which may be harmful and illegal or not at all.

A brief description of the Internet and its impact is, however, essential before moving on to policy issues.

The Internet

What is the Internet?

Local computer networks are made of two or more computers attached to each other by cables. The Internet is often described as an international computer network of computer networks that allows different computer users to share information and communicate interactively. It has no fixed physical location, central control point or permanent intelligence.

The 1990s have witnessed the emergence of an information society in which the Internet plays the leading role. Although the Internet has its roots in the early 1960s, it only emerged as a powerful, popular and user-friendly communications system in the early 1990s when it became more accessible to individuals not affiliated with military, government, research or academic organisations. The Internet is mainly an open environment and its usage is all about information; it therefore facilitates the exchange and retrieval of information and encourages browsing by the users. However, it can also be addictive!

After the creation of the WWW by the Conseil Européen pour la Recherche Nucléaire in Switzerland in 1992, the Internet started to develop in an unprecedented way. Originally aimed at the high-energy physics community, the WWW spread to other areas and attracted much interest for its potential in user support, resource recovery, and many other areas which depend on collaborative and information sharing. The Web has extended quickly beyond the scientific and academic communities to include communications by individuals, non-profit organisations and businesses all over the world.

Following the creation of the WWW, the Internet became more user-friendly thanks to browsing tools such as Netscape and Internet Explorer. Together with the WWW, the use of electronic mail ('e-mail') became fashionable, and it is now in the process of taking the place of the telephone and fax, revolutionising global communications. The Internet is the only global system where access is localised and therefore cheaper than other communications systems such as telephones, mobile phones and fax machines.

The Internet is not only a tool for communication but carries hybrid capabilities with ready facilities making publishing more accessible. Breaking down traditional barriers, the Internet offers anyone with access to a phone line and a computer with a modem) the opportunity to become a publisher in the online world. According to a European Commission Action Plan of November 1997, 'the Internet has also become a powerful element in social, educational and cultural fields – empowering citizens and educators, lowering the barriers to the creation and the distribution of content, offering universal access to ever richer sources of digital information'.

The Internet provides a variety of resources and a vast amount of information on almost any subject imaginable. Anyone with access to the Internet may take advantage of a wide variety of communication and information retrieval methods. While the most commonly used communication system is e-mail (including mailing lists), the WWW is the most popular part of the Internet for the retrieval and dissemination of information including not only text but audio visual content. Apart from usage of the Web and e-mail, the Internet offers the possibility of engaging with other users through newsgroups via electronic messages and live chat rooms (for example, through Internet Relay Chat). The domain of the above Internet activities is sometimes referred to or known collectively as 'cyberspace', a nowhere location without any known borders but available to anyone with the means to access the Internet.

The term 'cyberspace' was first used by the science fiction writer William Gibson in *Neuramancer*. Gibson used 'cyber-space' to describe an abstract, visual environment in which computer users would navigate the global network of infor-mation services.

Users may also, for example, access data from the UK and US governments' information servers, or order wine from supermarkets, books from online bookstores and flowers from Hawaii, or engage in discussions about a vast range of issues including sex and pornography. Yes, pornography and sexually explicit content is available on the Internet together with discussion groups dedicated to sex. The next section will provide further information about the nature of sexually explicit content on the Internet.

Porn on the Net

Pornography has been the most controversial topic on the Internet since the Usenet discussion groups and WWW pages became popular with online users. There are more than 200 sex-related Usenet newsgroups and many WWW pages with sexually explicit content. These WWW sites and newsgroups are accessible through the Internet to any online user with an Internet account – except for some limitations, for example, within UK Higher Education: the Joint Academic Network (JANET) Acceptable Use Policy prohibits the use of JANET for obscene and libellous materials (see <http://www.ja.net/documents/use.html>).

Pornography ranges from soft-core magazines like *Playboy* to more explicit videos including hard-core films depicting sexual acts such as vaginal and anal intercourse, fellatio and cunnilingus – between persons of opposite genders as well as persons of the same gender. However, most of the pornography available through the Internet already exists in other media such as magazines and videos. Apart from the live sex shows (very expensive) that are provided through the Internet, the porn industry is just using the new technologies to deliver what it has been delivering for decades. Still, the Internet provides new opportunities for consumers of porn to access such online content within the privacy of their own homes.

You will normally be warned about the contents of commercial pornographic web sites and you will need to accept their 'Terms of Use'. The following is just one example:

'Adult Consent and Legal Verification: By entering this site I declare under penalty of perjury that I am at least 18 years of age and I consent to viewing adult-oriented material that I may be exposed to as a result of following any links on this site, and that it is legal to view such material in my country and/or state and/or locality and/or Internet connection.'

All sorts of pornography are available on the Internet in different formats. Although it is mainly pictures and text, the porn industry is moving towards the provision of video images and sound files within a pornographic context. These range from short animated movies and clips from existing porn films, to live sex chat, live striptease and live sex acts. Most of this kind of pornographic content is available through the WWW pages, and in most cases the users are expected to have their credit cards ready.

Furthermore, Usenet discussion groups and mailing lists make it possible to discuss sex-related subjects over the Internet. There are more than 30,000 Usenet discussion groups all around the world but only around 200 or so groups are sex-related, some of which carry socially valuable and legitimate discussions concerning, for example, homosexuality or sexual abuse.

There are also sex-related discussions on the Internet Relay Chat (IRC) channels where users in small groups or on private channels exchange messages and files. But, as with the Web and the Usenet, only a small fraction of the IRC channels are dedicated to sex.

There are discussion groups on abortion, bondage and discipline, sadomasochism, homosexuality, fetishism, bisexuality, prostitution, sexual customs and rites, reproduction, erotica, dating, AIDS and other sex health issues, sexual abuse and sex crimes.

How did the cyberporn debate start?

The House of Commons Home Affairs Committee described computer pornography as a new horror in 1994 with the wide circulation of pornography via computer diskettes and CD-ROMs in mind, but pornography on the Internet really hit the media in the summer of 1995 when *Time* magazine published a cover study entitled 'Cyberporn' ('On a screen near you: Cyberporn', *Time*, 3 July 1995), based on the controversial study 'Marketing Pornography on the Information Superhighway' by a certain Marty Rimm of the Carnegie Mellon University, Pittsburgh, Pennsylvania. Rimm's eighteen-month study claimed that 83.5% of the Usenet discussion groups contained pornographic images. The study was later found to be misleading because it was based upon the many adult-oriented Bulletin Board Systems (BBS) all around the US, not the Internet. Rimm's study was published in the *Georgetown Law Journal* (83, 6, 1995, pp. 1839–1934) and this gave his study undeserved credibility. A more accurate figure has been calculated by Hoffman and Novak (both associate professors and marketing co-directors for Project 2000 at Vanderbilt University), who point out that 'less than one half of 1% (3% of 11%) of the messages on the Internet are associated with newsgroups that contain pornographic imagery'. (See the critique of the Rimm study

BBS is a computer Bulletin Board System. This is not an Internet service but is a computer system (or systems) which can be accessed directly by telephone and it allows users of the same BBS to communicate to each other or download and upload files. The BBS were popular before the Internet service providers became widely available.

by Hoffman and Novak, <http://www2000.ogsm.vanderbilt.edu/novak/rimm.review.html>)

The international coverage of the study by *Time* gave a distorted impression of the content of the Internet and provided journalists, Christian fundamentalists, Senators and worried parents in the USA with a definitive study which proved their fears that the Internet is all about pornography. Furthermore, Senator James Exon relied on the study for the approval of the Communications Decency Act in the USA. Although discredited by academia, the Rimm study and the *Time* coverage did cause damage and started a moral panic which has yet to come to an end. The damage was not only done within the USA; the effects of the international coverage soon emerged in other countries, including the UK. Wallace and Mangan point out

Sex, Laws and Cyberspace is written by Jonathan Wallace and Mark Mangan. Wallace, a graduate of Harvard Law School, was a plantiff in the successful *ACLU v. Reno* case which overturned the indecency provisions of the US Communications Decency Act 1996 (CDA). Mangan is a technology writer and web producer.

the irony in an update of *Sex, Laws and Cyberspace*
(Henry Holt & Company, 1996) that 'some people are still
passing around statistics from the Rimm study'. It is an
unfortunate legacy of Rimm's controversial story.

Cyberporn, or Internet pornography, remains a major
political issue on the Internet. Some argue strongly against
any form of pornography, claiming that it is harmful to women.
According to the professor of law (University of Michigan Law
School) and anti-pornography activist, Catharine MacKinnon,
'pornography in cyberspace is pornography in society, just
broader, deeper, worse, and more of it' ('Vindication and
Resistance: A Response to the Carnegie Mellon Study of
Pornography in Cyberspace', [*Georgetown Law Journal* 83,
6, 1995, p. 1959]). MacKinnon's definition of pornography in
cyberspace, however, reflects her own views on
pornography. For others, pornography is an issue of freedom
of speech and deserves the highest protection from
governmental regulation, as confirmed by the US Supreme
Court in *ACLU v. Reno* in 1997.

The pornography and harm debate

Whether pornography is harmful or not remains an issue
that has been hotly debated for decades. In 1970, the US
Commission on Obscenity and Pornography concluded
that the findings of empirical research on the effects of
pornography were insufficient to establish that pornography
is a central causal factor in acts of sexual violence. On this
basis the Commission recommended the repeal of many
laws that restricted adult access to sexually explicit material.
The findings of the Williams Committee in 1979 within the
UK were similar. The Committee admitted that any
presumption in favour of freedom of speech that may apply
to obscene publications would be displaced if it were

shown that they cause harm. In the USA, in 1986, the Meese Commission on Pornography concluded that 'the available evidence strongly supports the hypothesis that substantial exposure to sexually violent materials as described here bears a causal relationship to antisocial acts of violence and, for some subgroups, possibly to unlawful acts of sexual violence', although the Commission's findings are quite controversial and do not follow the earlier findings on pornography. The study was widely criticised at the time. In 1990, the UK Home Office Research and Planning Unit commissioned Dennis Howitt and Guy Cumberbatch to write the report *Pornography: Impacts and Influences*. The report concluded that there was no evidence of any causal links between pornography and sexual violence.

See the following documents for further information on the mentioned reports:
- United States Commission Report on Obscenity and Pornography (Washington, D.C., US Goverment Printing Office, 1970)
- Williams Committee Report, *Obscenity and Film Censorship* (London, HMSO, 1979)
- Attorney General's Commission on Pornography: Final Report, 2 vols (Washington, D.C., US Goverment Printing Office, 1986 [The Messe Commission])
- Howitt, D. and Cumberbatch, G., *Pornography: Impacts and Influences* (London, HMSO, 1990)

Pornography versus free speech

Some have sought to define the pornography debate as a free speech issue. Sexually explicit content does include images and text, and therefore it is natural to see such publications as a form of speech, and regulations and restrictions upon such speech as amounting to censorship of free expression. Evidently, the word 'speech' is not treated too literally where freedom of speech is concerned, and paintings, drawings and cartoons are certainly included. In the US, cross burning and flag abuse are also protected forms of speech under the First Amendment. Apart from free speech issues, others have argued that the consumption of pornography involves privacy issues, claiming that it should be the choice of individuals and consenting adults whether to consume such legal materials. Nadine Strossen, president of the American Civil Liberties Union, argues in *Defending Pornography: Free Speech, Sex and the Fight For Women's Rights* (New York, Scribner, 1995) that 'to suppress speech because it depicts the subordination of women would be as antithetical to central First Amendment principles as suppressing speech that depicts – or, indeed, even advocates – the subordination of racial minorities'. Pornography, it has been argued, may also be seen as an aid to individual fulfilment and personal identification.

In *R v. Anderson* (1971), the editors and publishing company of *OZ* magazine were indicted on counts of conspiracy to corrupt public morals by producing a magazine containing obscene items (such as Rupert Bear with an erection) contrary to the Obscene Publications Act 1959. Their convictions were quashed on appeal.

There have been serious attempts to ban all kinds of pornography by some of the pro-censorship feminists such as Catharine MacKinnon and Andrea Dworkin. In

1983 they drafted a model anti-pornography law which was passed by the Minneapolis City Council. In it, MacKinnon and Dworkin defined pornography as 'the sexually explicit subordination of women through pictures and/or words'. They declared that pornography is a practice of sex discrimination, but the proposed legislation was vetoed. In 1992, MacKinnon and Dworkin were successful in their campaign, but not in the US. The Canadian Supreme Court, in *R v. Butler*, accepted their views with respect to pornography. However, the *Butler* decision has been used predominantly against publications with a feminist or lesbian/gay orientation.

Andrea Dworkin's *Pornography: Men Possessing Women* and *Women Hating* were found to be obscene and seized by the Canadian Customs. According to the Customs, they illegally eroticised pain and bondage. But books such as Madonna's *Sex* and Bret Easton Ellis's *American Psycho* were not affected by the *Butler* decision.

Free speech in the UK?

There is no express constitutional guarantee for freedom of speech in the UK because of the absence of a comprehensive Bill of Rights, so its regulation depends upon common law and specific parliamentary legislation. In other words, the freedom exists where statute or common law rules do not restrict it. Although the European Convention on Human Rights (ECHR), which protects the freedom of expression in Article 10, does bind the UK in international law as an external bill of rights, it has not been directly implemented in the national laws. This situation is, however, set to change following the enactment of the Human Rights Act 1998 which will incorporate the ECHR into the English legal system. Such rights as freedom of expression will have statutory recognition, even though the ECHR has its limitations in Article 10(2). The European Court of Human Rights, in the *Handyside* case (1976), stated that the steps necessary in a democratic society for the protection of morals will depend on the type of morality to which a country is committed.

In conclusion, both the US and UK show in their approaches to pornography that it is at least arguable that pornography is within the concept of free speech because it may contain ideas and may be fulfilling, especially for consenting adults in their private lives, in ways which do not cause harm to others. Free speech has at times been suggested to be a good in itself, without need of further justification. People, the theory goes, will not be able to develop intellectually and spiritually unless they are free to formulate their beliefs and political attitudes through public discussion, and in response to the criticisms of others. Self-fulfilment is for each individual to conceive personally, and each can decide what constitutes a good life. Free speech may be a necessary component to achieve that good life, so governments should be required to give people the chance of self-fulfilment.

This is not to say that all kinds of pornography are justifiable. If the production of pornography involves harm, for instance to children, then it may be outlawed. Following the identification of these issues in relation to the Internet, this guide will now explore them in more detail.

UK Porn Wars

According to the Home Office Annual Report 1997, 'the issue of obscenity causes considerable public concern and controversy. Anxiety may focus on matters as diverse as violent computer games, the availability of sexually explicit material in newsagents, or the use of pornography by paedophiles.' Although the UK government, and in particular the Home Office, aims to ensure that 'a proper balance is maintained between the rights of adults to have access to certain material and protecting the most vulnerable in our society, especially children, from exposure to possibly harmful material', 'access to certain material' remains a very restrictive category for British adults.

In dealing with the availability of computer pornography and its presence over the Internet, the UK government favours a mixture of statutory controls and self-regulation. Indeed, Parliament amended the existing laws on obscenity with the Criminal Justice and Public Order Act in 1994 so as to include technological developments and to cover computer pornography. The 1994 Act also strengthened police powers to investigate pornography offences and increased the maximum penalties for transgressions of the child pornography laws. Although the laws have been amended and tightened to take into account technological changes, the state of obscenity laws within England and Wales remains unclear.

Obscene Publications Act 1959

The most cited and used law within England and Wales in relation to sexually explicit content and pornography is the 1959 Obscene Publications Act. The 1959 legislation is far more restrictive than comparable laws in any other European Union country and laws and regulations in the United States. The situation was even worse before 1959 with one 'purple passage' being enough to ban a publication completely. Between 1868 and 1959, the law courts applied the *Hicklin* obscenity test (1868) with the result that D. H. Lawrence's *The Rainbow* was destroyed in 1915 as well as *The Well of Loneliness* in 1928.

Hicklin Obscenity Test

The test in *R v. Hicklin* (1868) was based on the harm principle and Lord Chief Justice Cockburn defined the test of obscenity as 'whether the tendency of the matter charged as obscenity is to deprave and corrupt those whose minds are open to such immoral influences, and into whose hands a publication of this sort may fall.'

For a brief history of the UK obscenity laws see Robertson, G. and Nicol, A. *Media Law* (third edition, London, Penguin Books, 1992).

With the introduction of the Obscene Publications Act in 1959 a very large measure of freedom for 'written materials' was secured. Cases involving *Lady Chatterley's Lover*, *Last Exit to Brooklyn* and *Inside Linda Lovelace* illustrated the freedom given by the 1959 Act. Obscenity legislation within England and Wales was amended in 1994 to take into account sexually explicit content in computer data format, as mentioned above, but still, the applicability of UK obscenity standards to a borderless medium like the Internet has its difficulties and limitations. It is also questionable whether such national standards should be enforced on a global medium as these may affect the rights of others in other countries.

Section 1(1) of the 1959 Obscene Publications Act provides that 'an article shall be deemed to be obscene if its effect or the effect of any one of its items is, if taken as a whole, such as to tend to deprave and corrupt persons who are likely, having regard to all relevant circumstances, to read, see or hear the matter contained or embodied in it'. Section 1(2) of the Act makes it an offence to have an obscene article in ownership, possession or control with a view to publishing it for gain. The laws talk about publication for gain and distribution rather than mere possession. So, downloading porn from the Internet or viewing pornography on your screen may not amount to an illegality if you are not further distributing the content. But the same is not true for child pornography: if you are looking at child pornography through the Internet, even without downloading such content, you may be committing an offence.

It is normally the responsibility of the police to decide whether there are sufficient grounds to launch a criminal investigation under the above legislation, and that of the Crown Prosecution Service to decide whether to prosecute those alleged to be responsible for the publication and distribution. In practice, the enforcement of the Obscene Publications Act is directed towards hard-core and child pornography. Robertson and Nicol argue in *Media Law* (third edition, London, Penguin, 1992, p. 125) that 'nudity is now acceptable and even artistic, but to erect a penis is to provoke a prosecution' and this statement accurately summarises the state of obscenity laws within England and Wales. Furthermore, in practice the 1959 Act is not enforced within many regions and currently only three police forces have units dedicated to the investigation of obscene publications: the Metropolitan Police Service, Greater Manchester police and West Midlands police.

> 'The UK obscene publications units investigate the production and distribution of pornography, including pornography on the Internet, supervise licensed and unlicensed sex shops, supervise divisional obscene publication cases and provide advice in relation to obscene publication matters to other forces.'
>
> House of Commons, Hansard, Written Answers, 'Obscene Publications', 2 November 1998, column 386–7
>
> See <http://www.parliament.uk>

The police are also granted certain powers of search and seizure with respect to obscene articles with a warrant from a justice of the peace under section 3 of the Obscene Publications Act 1959.

In the case of obscene publications on the Internet, forfeiture proceedings often used by the police will not be applicable because of the nature of the Internet. Although the police may forfeit the computer equipment of UK offenders, they will not be able to do so if the potential offenders are outside the UK. Also, materials may be provided from a country where they are legal. For instance, although it is not possible to purchase the US edition of *Penthouse* magazine in the UK because it is considered obscene (or at least

West Midlands Police Paedophile and Pornography Squad confiscated a book of pictures by the photographer Robert Mapplethorpe from the University of Central England in Birmingham library and asked for permission to destroy it on the grounds of obscenity. However, the Crown Prosecution Service backed away in October 1998 acknowledging that the sexually explicit images could be defended as being 'for the public good' as a contribution to art or learning.

See <http://www.uce.ac.uk/mapplethorpe/index.html> for further details of this incident.

indecent under the Customs and Excise regulations), it is possible to access it on the Internet.

There have been many prosecutions and convictions under the obscene publications laws within England and Wales, although no individual statistics are available from the Home Office for obscene materials involving the Internet, as court proceedings data held centrally for offences under the Obscene Publications Act 1959 do not identify the type of medium used. As far as the Internet and obscene publications are concerned, there has not been much police activity, apart from the extensive police operations on child pornography.

It should be noted, however, that Customs and Excise is enforcing and controlling the physical entry of obscene and indecent materials into the UK jurisdiction. Section 42 of the Customs and Consolidation Act 1876 prohibits the importation into the UK of indecent or obscene prints, paintings, photographs, books, lithographic cards or other engravings, or any other indecent or obscene articles. This is because it is up to the European Union member states to invoke Article 36 of the Treaty establishing the

European Community to restrict imports of material on the grounds of public morality. In addition to the Customs' enforcement on physical content, the UK government has taken action against four satellite channels with adult-oriented content, namely Eurotica Rendez-Vous, Red Hot Television, TV Erotica and Satisfaction Club TV.

In a rare Internet-related case in March 1996, Jason Manger, author of the *Internet Bible*, was sentenced to one year's imprisonment (suspended) and was ordered to pay £1,000 costs. Manger was selling hard-core pornographic material to customers all around the world. He pleaded guilty to four charges of possessing an obscene article in order to publish it for profit. The judge likened the case to 'a blue movies mail order business using new technology'.

In another rare case, a twenty-one-year-old Lancashire University student pleaded guilty to four charges of publishing obscene articles on the Internet, contrary to the Obscene Publications Act, and another six of making indecent photographs of children, contrary to the Protection of Children Act 1978. 'S' was arrested following a joint inquiry between the Lancashire force and the Metropolitan Police's Vice Unit in January 1998. S had linked his UK-based web pages to a US-based web site which carried the obscene publications. Although the linking issue is debatable – and whether it amounts to publication is not clear – the police discovered that the US-based pages were also owned by the defendant. However, the case

Note that a UK citizen who publishes information about child sex tourism on a web site or who links to a web page dealing with this kind of information may well be prosecuted under the Sexual Offences (Conspiracy & Incitement) Act 1996.

does not set a precedent as the issues were not discussed within the court following S's guilty plea.

With the arbitrary application of national laws, the development of global communications systems and recent calls for a relaxation of obscenity standards, obscenity laws almost inevitably remain difficult to interpret with any authority. Many organisations and campaigns do argue against the restrictive and censorious laws and regulations within the UK. These include the likes of the National Campaign for the Reform of the Obscene Publications Acts (<http://freespace.virgin.net/old.whig /NCROPA/>), Feminists Against Censorship (<http://www. fiawol.demon.co.uk/FAC/>), and the Sexual Freedom Coalition (information <http://www.sfc.org.uk/>). These more traditional organisations are joined by the likes of Internet Freedom (<http://www.netfreedom.org/>), Campaign Against Censorship of the Internet in Britain (<http://www.liberty.org.uk/cacib/>), and Cyber-Rights & Cyber-Liberties (UK) (<http://www.cyber-rights.org>).

More recently, James Ferman, the outgoing president of the British Board of Film Classification (BBFC), said if explicit material were legalised it would be easier to regulate ('Porn film industry is out of control', *Daily Telegraph*, 8 August 1998). Ferman was referring to a relaxation of the obscenity laws on some forms of adult pornography which can be obtained through the black market within the UK.

Self-regulatory approach

At present, there are no plans to relax the current obscenity standards within the UK and there are also no initiatives to introduce any new regulatory measures to deal with the availability of sexually explicit content through the Internet.

BBFC Annual Report 1997–1998

In response to a steady increase in the public's tolerance of screen sex, confirmed by a wide range of research, the Board relaxed its stringent standards to allow marginally more explicitness in sex videos sold through licensed sex shops. This move was promptly curtailed when it became apparent that these standards were out of line with those of enforcement agencies such as Customs and Excise and the police and magistrates' courts. In October 1998, the Board reverted to its previous standards, but it is concerned that the failure to distinguish between harmful forms of pornography and those which are merely offensive will fuel the already flourishing black market which mixes pornography with obscenity. Mr Ferman says that this is one of the biggest problems he leaves for his successors and calls for a solution to be found.

There appears to be no single solution for the regulation on a worldwide basis of illegal and harmful content on the Internet. Therefore, the government appears to prefer the self-regulatory approach advocated by the European Union which includes the creation of hotlines to report illegal content, rating and filtering systems for the category of legal content which may be offensive or harmful, for example to children, a code of practice for the Internet service providers, and awareness programmes to educate those who are in care of children, especially parents and teachers.

Self-regulation may be a suitable approach as it would allow adaptability in tune with technological changes and with the development of the Internet. Self-regulation is also more easily 'internalised' – seen as appropriate by those to whom it applies and therefore more likely to be observed rather than evaded.

Self-regulation does not completely exclude national government legal regulation. For example, national government bodies would be needed for the enforcement of existing laws. However, many argue that the UK government and the European Union have chosen the wrong tools for a self-regulatory environment for the Internet. Many observers, including civil liberties organisations, are sceptical about private policing initiatives such as the setting-up of hotlines to report illeagal Internet content and the development of rating and filtering systems.

In November 1997, the European Commission adopted a new proposal for an action plan, promoting the safe use of the Internet. The action plan proposed by the European Commission concentrated on the regulation of illegal and harmful content on the Internet and the UK government welcomed the initiative with its emphasis on self-regulation by industry as entirely consistent with the UK's approach: 'The UK strongly agrees with the [European] Commission that since a legal framework for regulation of the Internet already exists in Member States, new laws or regulations are unnecessary' (House of Commons, Select Committee on European Legislation, Fourth Report [London, HMSO, .1996]). More recently, Chris Smith, the Secretary of State for National Heritage, stated:

It should be noted that for legal content which can be unsuitable for young people, the UK government supports non-statutory schemes such as the voluntary Code of Practice under which newsagents refuse to sell adult magazines to persons under the age of 18, and the Teenage Magazine Arbitration Panel which oversees a binding set of guidelines on how editors of teenage magazines should deal with sexual matters.

It is vital, however, in considering how best to
address [the problem of illegal and harmful content on
the Internet], that we bear in mind that only a small
fraction of the material available to the public poses a
threat to the protection of minors or human dignity. It
will be important, therefore, not to impose hasty
regulation upon these new services and thereby
constrain their development and the educational,
commercial and social opportunities and other
benefits they can engender.

**House of Commons, Select Committee on European Legislation,
Second Report (London, HMSO, 1997, HC 155-ii)**

The police response

Although the UK government supports self-regulation with
respect to Internet control, the UK police appear to want
to take a more pro-active regulatory role. In mid-August
1996, the Clubs and Vice Unit of the Metropolitan Police
sent a letter to the UK Internet service providers (ISPs)
supplying them with a list of Usenet discussion groups
they believed to contain pornographic material. The list
mainly covered newsgroups which carried child
pornography, but it also included other newsgroups,
which might or might not include sexually explicit content.

The action taken by the UK police appears to have
been ill-considered and did little to reduce the availability
of obscene material on the Internet. Furthermore, the list of
newsgroups provided by the UK police included much
material that is not illegal, such as legitimate discussion
groups for homosexuals, and discussion groups which
contain text, sexual fantasies and stories but no pictures.
These would almost certainly not infringe the Obscene
Publications Act. The action of the UK police also

amounted to censorship of material without public debate in Parliament or elsewhere. It is submitted that political action by the UK government would be preferable to random censorship by law enforcement authorities.

The panic over the Usenet discussion groups was followed by the setting up of an industry-based organisation, the Internet Watch Foundation (IWF), following discussions between the Home Office, the police, the Internet Service Providers' Associations (ISPA) and the London Internet Exchange (LINX).

At the time of writing this guide, the UK government remains 'determined to ensure that criminal law is effective in protecting people from harmful material and, with this in mind, keeps the obscenity legislation under review.'

House of Commons' Written Answers, 'Obscene Publications', 2 November 1998, column 386–7

See <http://www.parliament.uk>

Porn in the USA

There has been great concern about pornography as a free speech issue in the United States because of the protection freedom of speech enjoys under the First Amendment. US pornography laws differ from those in the UK because of this constitutional protection. US constitutional case law makes a distinction between obscene and indecent speech. While there is no First Amendment protection of obscene speech, indecent speech is protected, though with limitations where there is a sufficient government interest.

Following the moral panic regarding cyberporn, in February 1996 the US President signed the Telecommunications Act 1996 which included the provisions of the Communications Decency Act 1996 (CDA). The clear purpose of the CDA was to restrict access by minors to 'patently offensive depictions of sexual or excretory activities', that is to widely available pornographic images and materials online over an 'interactive computer service', including materials available on the Internet. Because of mass appeal and easy access by children, additional regulations were included to ensure a higher level of scrutiny in broadcasting than in print media within the United States. If part of a broadcasting programme on radio or on television is patently offensive, vulgar or shocking then it may be considered 'indecent' and banned at certain times of the day.

The CDA was controversial because it intended to restrict 'indecent speech' over the Internet, which can be accessed by adults, and it could easily have been applied to information involving, for example, birth control and abortion. The CDA was immediately challenged by the American Civil Liberties Union (ACLU – <http://www.aclu.org>) and other plaintiffs on the day it was signed into law by President Clinton, although plaintiffs did not challenge the statute to the extent that it covers obscenity or child pornography, which were already proscribed before the CDA's adoption.

The trial of the Internet

In *ACLU v. Reno*, ACLU claimed that the public would be irreparably harmed because their rights under the First Amendment would be infringed. ACLU also claimed that the CDA was ill-defined and hence that plaintiffs would not know what speech or other actions might subject them to prosecution. ACLU and the other plaintiffs argued:

> The Act bans all expression that is 'indecent' or 'offensive' from all online systems that are accessible to minors. Not only does this ban unconstitutionally restrict the First Amendment rights of minors and those who communicate with them about important issues, but, because of the nature of the online medium, it essentially bans 'indecent' or 'patently offensive' speech entirely, thus impermissibly reducing the adult population to 'only what is fit for children'.
> *ACLU, et al. v. Janet Reno* (929 F Supp 824, 1996)

The plaintiffs requested a temporary restraining order, and the court ordered that the plaintiffs' motion be granted in part only eight days after the CDA was signed. Judge Buckwalter concluded that 'this strikes me as being serious because the undefined word "indecent", standing alone, would leave reasonable people perplexed in evaluating what is or is not prohibited by the statute'.

The decision of the Federal District Court in
ACLU v. Reno

On 12 June 1996, a three-judge panel in the Federal District Court of Philadelphia held that the plaintiffs had established a reasonable probability of eventual success in the litigation by demonstrating that certain sections of the CDA were unconstitutional. The kind of 'indecency' identified as potentially criminal by government witnesses included Internet postings of the well-known photograph of the actress Demi Moore naked and pregnant on the cover of *Vanity Fair*.

The court wrote that communications over the Internet did not 'invade' an individual's home or appear on one's computer screen unbidden. Moreover, users seldom encountered content 'by accident'. Almost all sexually explicit images are preceded by warnings as to the content, the court stated. Judge Dalzell stated that: 'As the most participatory form of mass speech yet developed, the Internet deserves the highest protection from government intrusion. Just as the strength of the Internet is chaos, so the strength of our liberty depends upon the chaos and cacophony of the unfettered speech the First Amendment protects.'

The decision of the Philadelphia court was an important step for freedom of speech on the Internet, but not a conclusive one as it was only a preliminary injunction.

The decision of the Supreme Court in *ACLU v. Reno*

The battle for free speech on the Internet continued in the US Supreme Court in 1997 following the US government's appeal. On 26 June 1997, in an historic ruling determining the future of free speech on the Internet the Supreme Court struck down the online censorship provisions of the CDA by a 7:2 vote. The Supreme Court affirmed the Philadelphia court's ruling that the CDA was unconstitutional:

> The CDA's 'indecent transmission' and 'patently offensive display' provisions abridge 'the freedom of speech' protected by the First Amendment. As a matter of constitutional tradition, in the absence of evidence to the contrary, we presume that governmental regulation of the content of speech is more likely to interfere with the free exchange of ideas than to encourage it. The interest in encouraging freedom of expression in a democratic society outweighs any theoretical but unproven benefit of censorship.
> <http://www.aclu.org/court/renovacludec.html>

Existing US laws are adequate enough to deal with the problem of obscene materials and child pornography on the Internet as indicated by Judge Dalzell in the lower court of Philadelphia. The extension of the CDA to 'indecent speech' would have had a chilling effect on the Internet. Information regarding protection from AIDS, birth control, teenage pregnancy or prison rape is sexually explicit and may be considered 'indecent' or 'patently offensive' in some communities, and this kind of speech would have been affected by the provisions of the CDA. Legislation such as the CDA might have set up a dangerous precedent for similar legislation in modern and developing societies, including the UK.

However, the battle for free speech does not seem to be over as new legislation already dubbed 'CDAII' was introduced to the US Senate in 1998.

Child Online Protection Act

The Child Online Protection Act (COPA), enacted by the US Congress as part of an omnibus appropriations bill, would punish 'commercial' online distributors of material deemed 'harmful to minors' with up to six months in jail and a $50,000 fine. Following the enactment of this legislation, civil liberties organisations including the ACLU, Electronic Privacy Information Center (EPIC) and Electronic Frontier Foundation filed a court challenge in October 1998. David Sobel, EPIC's legal counsel, said that making children the excuse for ill-conceived censorship schemes was poor public policy. Moreover, Mr Sobel called for finding ways to protect both children and the First Amendment on the day the challenge was filed. Furthermore, in a statement issued on 21 October 1998, the Global Internet Liberty Campaign (GILC) criticised the US's attempts to introduce censorious legislation and stated:

> the COPA will not be effective in keeping from minors material that might be inappropriate for them. No criminal provision will be more effective than efforts to educate parents and minors about Internet safety and how to properly use online resources. Moreover, we note again that the Internet is a global medium. Despite all the enforcement efforts that might be made, a national censorship law cannot protect children from online content they will always be able to access from sources outside of the United States.
> <http://www.cyber-rights.org/gilc/gilc-cda.htm>

GILC (<http://www.gilc.org>) is a coalition of international organisations founded in 1996 to defend civil liberties and human rights on the Internet. The GILC statement on the COPA is at <http://www.cyber-rights.org/gilc/gilc-cda.htm>

On 19 November 1998, Judge Lowell A. Reed Jr. stated that the plaintiffs had shown 'a likelihood of success on the merits of at least some of their claims' that the COPA violated the First Amendment rights of adults. Significantly, the judge emphasised that the temporary restraining order applied to all Internet users, not just the plaintiffs in the case. In February 1999 Judge Reed blocked COPA, stating that it would restrict free speech in the 'marketplace of ideas'. In granting a preliminary injunction against COPA, the judge held that the plaintiffs were likely to succeed on their claim that the law 'imposes a burden on speech that is protected for adults'. (See the February 1999 decision of Judge Reed at <http://www.aclu.org/court/acluvrenoII_pi_order.html>)

So the battle continues within the USA while the rest of the world is watching. Keep an eye on <http://www.epic.org/free_speech/copa/> to follow this case in detail.

European Porn
Union?

There have been Internet content-related problems in Britain, Germany and elsewhere in Europe during the last couple of years. Some material, such as pornography and hate speech, is usually considered to be harmful, especially to children and vulnerable minorities. Although there is a strong commitment based on global economic competition and, equally, political populism to embrace in principle the age of the information society, there will inevitably be divergent approaches to the growth and governance of the Internet in different European societies because of cultural, historical and socio-political diversity.

For example, while the German government has political fears and sensitivities about the use of the Internet by neo-Nazis, the United Kingdom takes a more relaxed attitude to the dangers of racism but conversely has a long cultural tradition of repressing sexually explicit material, as discussed earlier. There are differences within the general and specific laws of each European Union member state in relation to obscene publications and child pornography. The differences depend upon the cultural, moral, political and legal traditions of each individual member state. While material that would be considered obscene within the UK is legally available to adults in

Germany, Italy and other European Union member states, laws may prohibit in those countries the availability of such content to children.

Germany did clarify its laws in relation to Internet service providers' liability, but that did not prevent the Felix Somm prosecution in May 1998. According to the German Teleservices Act 1997, 'Internet service providers can be held accountable for illegal material on their services only if they know about the content and blocking or removing the content in question is technically possible'.

CompuServe Germany Case

Felix Somm, the ex-general manager for CompuServe in Germany, was found guilty of having assisted in the dissemination of pornographic writings in thirteen legally coinciding cases. Somm received a two-year suspended sentence and a fine of DM100,000 from the Munich district court in May 1998.

See the decision in the Felix Somm case at <http://www.cyber-rights.org/isps/somm-dec.htm>

In most cases, public opinion is the determining factor where the protection of children and sensitive issues such as paedophilia are involved. Although there are minor cultural differences between the member states, the availability of child pornography over the Internet is one of the main reasons why the European Union has been involved with Internet regulation, even though illegality and criminal law remains within the supremacy of the individual member states. In the summer of 1996, the Belgian government appealed for international co-operation to crush paedophile rings as it sought to defuse the nation's fury over the Marc Dutroux affair, and this call tied up with other calls during 1996 within Europe, triggering the European Commission initiatives. Austria has also welcomed all initiatives to create an applicable international legal framework. In July 1998, during its presidency of the European Union, the Austrian government called for action against child pornography following the discovery of a paedophilia ring using the Internet in the Netherlands. This followed calls by the ex-German Chancellor Helmut Kohl for stronger international co-operation in the struggle against child pornography, again in July 1998.

The Internet is a global medium and material originates in a variety of countries and is accessible to any user connected to the Internet. It was the European Union's task, then, to try to reflect these differences in its proposals.

Taking into account these difficulties and differences, the European Commission launched its Action Plan for the safe use of the Internet in November 1997.

Finally, following over a year of discussions within the institutions of the European Union, in December 1998 the Council of the European Union approved the Action Plan's aim of promoting safer use of the Internet by combating illegal and harmful content on global networks. The name of the Action Plan was changed slightly from 'safe use of the Internet' to 'safer use of the Internet'. Members of the European Parliament (MEPs) thought that employing the words 'safer use' would be more appropriate since the EU legislation did not cover criminal law and it would not be an easy task to promote 'safe' Internet use. Furthermore, according to the MEPs, it was illusory to believe that the Action Plan alone could eliminate illegal and harmful material on the Internet. However, the MEPs agreed that the adoption of the Action Plan was a step in the right direction.

Details of the EU Action Plan

Decision No. /98/EC of the European Parliament and of the Council of adopting a Multiannual Community Action Plan on promoting safer use of the Internet by combating illegal and harmful content on global networks, December 1998, can be found at <http://www2.echo.lu/legal/en/internet/actplan.html>

The new Action Plan recognised that the Internet does not exist in a 'legal vacuum'. However, because of the global nature of the Internet the EU prefers self-regulatory solutions for the control of illegal and harmful material on the Internet.

The Situation in Ireland

Ireland has a long history of censorship laws and is known for strict pornography regulations in other media. Some very stringent controls exist, and there has been a broad acceptance of censorship for many years. Books such as *The Joy of Sex* and *The Erotic Art of India* were censored or banned by the Irish Censorship of Publications Board in 1987. It has only recently become legal to import publications known for pornographic content, such as the *Playboy* magazine.

However, a recent working party report stated that 'traditional forms of censorship will not operate in the new borderless virtual environment of the Internet'. According to the report, the Internet Service Providers Association of Ireland will play a key role in establishing a safe environment for children online. The self-regulatory approach favoured by the Irish group parallels the European Union Action Plan.

For the Irish approach to the Internet, see the Irish Department of Justice, Equality and Law Reform report, *Illegal and Harmful Use of the Internet* (Pn. 5231, Dublin, 1998, pp. 33–35).

The Action Plan encourages the creation of a European network of hotlines for online users to report illegal content such as child pornography; the development of self-regulatory and content-monitoring schemes by content and access providers; the development of internationally compatible and interoperable rating and filtering schemes to protect users; and measures to increase awareness of the possibilities available among parents, teachers, children and other consumers to help these groups to use the networks while choosing the appropriate content and exercising a reasonable amount of parental control. These initiatives take place between 1999 and 2002.

There are already active hotlines for reporting illegal content within the UK, the Netherlands, Austria, Belgium and Germany. The Irish government is already planning such a hotline based upon the UK model, but some member states remain sceptical about the introduction of such hotlines. The September 1998 French State Council report noted that this kind of hotline can be accepted only for very specific subjects such as paedophilia and incitement to racial hatred see <http://www.internet.gouv.fr/francais/textesref/rapce98/accueil.htm>. The report stated:

> It is essential to know who is managing the line and in accordance with what criteria. In this connection, although it is seemingly effective, the British arrangements for handling unlawful messages have provoked a lot of criticism on the grounds that it gives the hotline very wide prerogatives both with regard to classifying the content of the sites and the possibility of cutting access to them. Has an association of access providers this right? Is there not a risk of censorship or of substitution for the court?

Furthermore, codes of conduct for the Internet service providers are currently being established and developed within different European Union member states, and rating and filtering systems are backed by many governments as a way forward for dealing with harmful Internet content and for the sake of protecting children from such material.

While all these initiatives appear attractive to concerned users, there are certain matters which should be carefully addressed before developing the suggested EU solutions. Rating and filtering systems claim to empower users to block unwanted material from their personal systems. The most sophisticated and widely recognised of these systems is the Platform for Internet Content Selection, introduced by the World Wide Web Consortium. European governments were especially interested in this hoped-for self-regulatory solution to harmful Internet content.

Cyberporn and
Children

The availability of adult-oriented sexually explicit content on the Internet remains a matter of concern to some users, and especially to parents and those who care for children. This guide so far has shown that pornography is available on the Internet; however, Internet users have to actively look for it and nowadays most pornography is available as a commercial service and requires payment via credit cards. Commercial pornography and the requirement of credit-card payment means that, contrary to popular opinion, pornography is not freely available to minors through the WWW as theoretically the users have to be at least 18 years old to access such web sites. However, some pornography is available on the Internet without charge, especially through Usenet discussion groups and through those professional commercial web sites who use freebies to attract users.

It is important to note that the discussion here concerns adult pornography which is legal and therefore within the limits of national laws and regulations for consuming pornography. However, what should concerned users do if they do not want to access pornography on the Internet, or, moreover, what should they do if they are concerned about their children accessing pornography? According to some the answer is the usage of filtering and rating systems. This guide will now explain these systems, how they work and what they can and cannot do for you.

Rating systems

Platform for Internet Content Selections (PICS) is an Internet protocol for Internet rating systems and is similar to the V-chip technology for filtering out violence or pornography on television systems. PICS was developed by the Massachusetts Institute of Technology's World Wide Web Consortium and is widely supported to be an industry standard for Internet rating systems by various governments.

PICS works by embedding electronic labels in the text or image documents to vet their content before the computer displays them or passes them on to another computer. The vetting system could include sexually explicit, political, religious, advertising or commercial topics. These can be added by the publisher of the material, by the company providing access to the Internet, or by an independent vetting body.

Currently, there are three PICS-related rating systems that are being used or promoted.

RSACi

This is the best-known system (<http://www.rsac.org/>). It was developed by the US-based Recreational Software Advisory Council on the Internet, originally a scheme for rating computer games. It rates material according to the degree of sex, violence, nudity and bad language depicted. It is usually this PICS/RSACi screening combination that people have in mind when they refer to PICS, and this is the system preferred and promoted by

the UK's Internet Watch Foundation and is supported by
the government.

SafeSurf

SafeSurf is developed by the SafeSurf corporation
(<http://www.safesurf.com/>), and this system's categories
include 'Age Range', 'Profanity', 'Heterosexual Themes',
'Homosexual Themes', 'Nudity', 'Violence', 'Sex, Violence
and Profanity', 'Intolerance', 'Glorifying Drug Use', 'Other
Adult Themes', and 'Gambling', with nine distinctions for
each category. SafeSurf, for example, offered the US
House Judiciary Committee its assistance with the Internet
release of the Starr Report on President Clinton and
claimed that the report, which included sexually explicit
content, should be SafeSurf rated.

SafeSurf and RSACi both rely on self-rating of
Internet sites by web publishers. While apparently being
voluntary and fair, this kind of system is likely to end up
being a serious burden on content providers.

NetShepherd

NetShepherd is based in Calgary (<http://www.
netshepherd.com/>) and rates sites based on maturity
levels (general, child, pre-teen, teen, adult and
objectionable) and quality levels (1–5 stars). Unlike
SafeSurf and RSACi, NetShepherd conducts third-party
ratings of web sites.

See, for further information, Harry Hochheiser,
Computer Professionals for Social Responsibility Filtering
FAQ, Version 1.1.1, 24 October 1998, at <http://quark.
cpsr.org/~harryh/faq.html>

Filtering software

Most filtering software available is designed for the home
market. It is intended to respond to the preferences of
parents making decisions for their own children. There are
currently around forty blocking and filtering products and
these are mainly US-based (<http://www.netparents.org/
parentstips/browsers.html>) and do not represent the cultural
differences in a global environment such as the Internet.

It has been reported many times that this kind of
software is over-inclusive and limits access to or censors
inconvenient web sites, or filters potentially educational
materials regarding AIDS and drug abuse prevention.
Therefore, 'censorware' enters homes despite the hype
over 'parental control' as an alternative to government
censorship. The companies creating this kind of software
also provide no appeal system to content providers who
are 'banned', thereby 'subverting the self-regulating
exchange of information that has been a hallmark of the
Internet community.' (Computer Professionals for Social
Responsibility letter, December 1996, at <http://www.cpsr.
org/cpsr/nii/cyber-rights/>)

Government support for such technologies

In February 1998, the Internet Watch Foundation (IWF), a
self-regulatory body supported by the UK government,
announced its consultation paper for the development of
rating systems at a national level. According to an IWF
press release, rating systems would 'meet parents'
concerns about Internet content that is unsuitable for
children'. The consultation document by the IWF did not
discuss whether these systems were suitable for the UK or
whether they were needed at all. For a critique of the IWF

proposals, see Cyber-Rights & Cyber-Liberties (UK) Report: 'Who Watches the Watchmen: Part II – Accountability & Effective Self-Regulation in the Information Age', September 1998, at <http://www.cyber-rights.org/watchmen-ii.htm>

> 'The IWF is working with Internet service providers to ensure that, before their users place new material on the Internet, they provide it with a contents rating which can be identified by the latest computer software. This should help Internet users, especially parents, to control the material coming into their homes. The government is monitoring closely the success of this system.'
>
> **Home Office Annual Report 1997 'Obsenity Issues', The Stationary Office, Cm 3608**
>
> See < http://www.homeoffice.gov.uk/obsene.htm>

According to John Battle, Minister for Science, Energy and Industry, 'such ratings and filtering tools can be extremely useful in helping parents and other adults who care for children to decide on the types of legal material they wish their children to access' (HMG Strategy for the Internet: Memorandum by the Hon. John Battle, House of Commons, 18 March 1998, at <http://www.dti.gov.uk/Minspeech/btlspch3.htm>).

A decision has already been taken by the IWF to develop these systems and its consultation paper addresses how this can be done. The paper's set of recommendations illustrates the IWF's position: rating systems are good and should be developed for use in this country.

The arbitrary decision taken by the IWF consultation document is supported and encouraged by the UK government and by members of Parliament. For example, Mr Alun Michael of the Home Office stated:

> Filtering software packages, such as Net Nanny, are available which enable parents to deny access to material containing sexually explicit words. Building on this, a working group of representatives from the IWF and Internet Service Providers has been devising a common ratings system suitable for UK Internet users on which there is growing international co-operation. This system is expected to address legal, but potentially offensive, material without curtailing freedom of expression.
> **House of Commons, Hansard, Written Answers, 18 February 1998, column 678**

Therefore, it would be correct to say that it is the policy of the UK government to develop such systems. However, these systems are less than perfect and they can be used for the exclusion of socially useful web sites and information. The following section will address these concerns associated with rating and filtering systems, which have not been addressed so far by the IWF or by the government and the European Union.

Defective systems

Rating and filtering systems have been part of an ongoing Internet controversy and have been widely criticised by civil liberties organisations as such systems may be the perfect tool for cyber-censorship. It seems that there are problems related to the use of rating systems and filtering software not necessarily addressed by both national and international initiatives. Far from empowering individual users or supervisors (such as parents), systems such as PICS are reliant upon a centralised system of classification of material content. But this classification process clearly takes control away from end-users and imposes standards which most do not have the time, inclination or knowledge to question (or even notice). The classification process also imposes forms of cultural hegemony which are most undesirable. What is illegal and harmful depends on cultural differences, and there are significant variations in different societies. It is therefore imperative that international initiatives take into account different ethical standards in different countries in order to arrive at appropriate rules to protect people against offensive material.

In August 1997, the ACLU was alarmed because of the failure to examine the longer-term implications for the Internet of rating and blocking schemes. The ACLU published a white paper in August 1997 entitled 'Fahrenheit 451.2: Is Cyberspace Burning? How Rating and Blocking Proposals May Torch Free Speech on the Internet' (<http://www.aclu.org/issues/cyber/burning.html>). The paper warned that government-coerced industry efforts to rate content on the Internet could destroy free speech online. The ACLU paper stated that 'in the physical world, people censor the printed word by burning books. But in the virtual world, you can just as easily censor controversial speech by banishing it to the farthest corners of cyberspace with blocking and rating schemes.' According to the ACLU, third-party rating systems pose free speech problems, and with few third-party rating products currently available, the potential for arbitrary censorship increases.

In December 1997, the Electronic Privacy Information Center (EPIC) released 'Faulty Filters: How Content Filters Block Access to Kid-Friendly Information on the Internet' (<http://www2.epic.org/reports/filter-report.html>) to determine the impact of software filters on the open exchange of information on the Internet. EPIC conducted a hundred searches using a traditional search engine (AltaVista search engine at <http://altavista.digital.com>) and then conducted the same hundred searches using a new search engine advertised as the 'world's first family-friendly Internet search site' (Net Shepherd Family Search at <http://family.netshepherd.com>). In every case in their sample searches, EPIC found that the family-friendly search engine prevented them from obtaining access to almost 90 per cent of the materials on the Internet containing the relevant search terms. For example, a search term including National Association for the Advancement of Coloured People resulted in 4,076 hits with the AltaVista search engine, while the same search term resulted in just fifteen hits with the NetShepherd Family Search, which meant that 99.6 per cent of the material was filtered out.

The EPIC study shows that the would-be family-friendly technologies can be very hostile and result in censorship of socially acceptable and legal content. The Wisdom Fund (<http://www.twf.org>), which promotes social justice and interfaith understanding by disseminating The Truth About Islam, was, for example, blocked by I-Gear, a filtering software in a test conducted by Peacefire (<http://www.peacefire.org/censorware/I-Gear>). I-Gear also blocked Cyber-Rights & Cyber-Liberties (UK) pages for a while and put it under the 'adult category' although the web pages have no adult content. (For further information, see Wallace, Jonathan, et al, 'The Censorware Project' at <http://www.censorware.org/>)

It is well known that these filtering tools are also used to exclude speech related to sexual minority groups. These kinds of filtering software normally include informational sites serving the lesbian, gay, bisexual and transgender community in the same categories as sexually explicit sites. (Gay & Lesbian Alliance Against Defamation report, 'Access Denied: The Impact of Internet Filtering Software on the Lesbian and Gay Community' <http://www.glaad. org/glaad/access_denied/index.html>, December 1997.)

Furthermore, in June 1998, the ACLU stated in a new report entitled 'Censorship in a Box: Why Blocking Software is Wrong for Public Libraries' that the mandatory use of Internet-blocking software in libraries is inappropriate and unconstitutional. The report comes as more and more US librarians are being pressured to install such software on library terminals to prevent minors from accessing objectionable materials. (<http://www.aclu.org/issues/ cyber/box.html>)

ACLU, in November 1998, successfully challenged the Loudoun County Library in Virginia for unconstitutionally restricting online access by using filtering systems. The decision of a federal district court in Virginia stated that 'any library policy that censors adults in the guise of protecting minors is unconstitutional', and 'mandatory blocking constitutes "prior restraint" – an extreme form of censorship that few courts have allowed' within the USA.

In July 1998, the Economic and Social Committee of the European Commission published its opinion on the EU Action Plan. The Committee considered it highly unlikely that the proposed measures would, in the long term, result in a safe Internet with the rating and classification of all information on the Internet being 'impracticable'. One of the dangers of this approach noted by the Committee was that the use of filtering tools might create a false sense of security for parents and teachers, while children would quickly find any loopholes. The Committee further questioned the claim that PICS could turn the Internet into an environment free of harmful content. More importantly, the Committee was worried that the possibility of Internet service providers using filtering and rating systems at the level of entry would render these systems, dubbed 'user empowering', an instrument of control, 'actually taking choice out of citizens' hands'.

Filtering software and rating systems, therefore, can be and will be used to exclude minority views and gripe sites rather than protecting children from anything. The Internet remains a wonderful resource for online users including children, and it should be their parents' responsibility to control what they access. Any regulatory action intended to protect a certain group of people, such as children, should not take the form of an unconditional prohibition of using the Internet to distribute content that is freely available to adults in other media. The US Supreme Court stated in *ACLU v. Reno* (1997) that 'the Internet is not as "invasive" as radio or television' and confirmed the finding of the US Court of Appeal that 'communications over the Internet do not "invade" an individual's home or appear on one's computer screen unbidden'.

So, the technology discussed in this chapter does not provide ideal solutions for the relatively small problems created by harmful Internet content. Relying on such technologies only provides a false sense of security for concerned users, parents and those in their care. Perhaps it would be better for parents to educate their children rather than placing their trust in technology or in an industry that believes it can do a better job of protecting children than they can.

The Problem of
Child Pornography

A primary concern of governments, regulators and law enforcement bodies in relation to illegal Internet content has been the availability of child pornography. This has been the case ever since paedophiles started to use the Internet for circulating pornographic materials related to children. Paedophilia networks have been using computer networks since as early as 1986, and references to child pornography were made on local computer bulletin board systems in the UK as early as 1985. The search for solutions can be traced within the UK to events starting with Operation Starburst in 1995, while the decision of the European Union to take firm action can be linked to the Marc Dutroux affair in Belgium in 1996.

Child pornography is a form of sexual abuse and exploitation in which the depiction of children engaging in sexually explicit conduct poses a serious threat to the physical and mental health, safety and well-being of children. Images of child pornography are seen as a permanent record of the victim's abuse, and its creation and distribution is considered a serious crime in most countries. Possession of child pornography is normally a lesser offence, while in some countries it is not an offence to possess child pornography.

Recent years have also seen a trend towards criminalising the production and possession of indecent pseudo-photographs of children in which there is no direct harm to children during production. Pseudo-photographs are technically photographs, but they are created by computer software manipulating one or more pre-existing pictures. For example, a child's face can be superimposed on an adult body, or another child's body, with the characteristics of the body altered to create pornographic computer-generated images without the involvement of a real child. Although there is no direct harm to children, such images may be used for 'grooming' children into child pornography and sexual activity, and on that basis there is justification for creating a new form of criminal by making it an offence to produce such images.

How big is the problem over the Internet?

Paedophilia networks operate underground and their activities are largely hidden, so it is impossible to assess the real extent of the problem. It is clear, however, that the problem mainly exists within the newsgroups; the situation on the World Wide Web is less clear. A study conducted at University College, Cork claims that the amount of child pornography accessible through the Internet is considerable, and that the situation is fluid and dynamic with sites frequently changing addresses. The study suggests that 0.07% of the 40,000 newsgroups carry 'child erotica' or 'pornography' (research carried out in January 1998), plus 238 'girl-related child pornography or erotica' web pages out of around fifty million web pages. (See a summary of the Cork Study in the Irish Department of Justice, Equality and Law Reform, *Illegal and Harmful Use of the Internet* [Pn. 5231, Dublin, 1998, pp. 33–35].)

The major problem for the future would be the availability of channels devoted to child pornography within the IRC or ICQ environment. The Cork study on this front concluded that 'due to the organised dynamic nature of paedophile activity it is not possible to estimate with accuracy the amount of traffic generated on IRC channels'. However, the definitions used within the Cork study are far from tight, and claims that this source of child pornography is either 'major' or 'increasing' are unsubstantiated in terms of absence of earlier studies or comparative investigations of other forms of trafficking.

UK laws dealing with child pornography

Protection of Children Act 1978

The 1978 Act was passed in response to the problem of child pornography. Its main purpose was to close some potential gaps in the measures available to police and prosecutors. The definition of 'photograph' given in the 1978 Act was extended to include photographs in electronic data format following the amendments made by the Criminal Justice and Public Order Act 1994.

The 1994 Act introduced the above-mentioned concept of 'pseudo-photographs' of children. It is now an offence under Section 1 of the 1978 Act 'for a person to take, or permit to be taken or to make, any indecent photographs or pseudo-photographs of a child; (or) to distribute or show such indecent photographs or pseudo-photographs'.

Section 160 of the Criminal Justice Act 1988

Under Section 160 of the 1988 Act, as amended by the Criminal Justice and Public Order Act 1994, it is an offence for a person to have an indecent photograph or pseudo-photograph of a child in his possession. This offence is now a serious arrestable transgression with a maximum imprisonment term not exceeding six months. It has been used in its new form in many cases involving possession of child pornography.

To have a defence under the 1988 Act, the defendant will have to prove under Section 160(2):

> (a) that he had a legitimate reason for having the photograph or pseudo-photograph in his possession; or
> (b) that he had not himself seen the photograph or pseudo-photograph and did not know, nor had any cause to suspect, it to be indecent; or
> (c) that the photograph or pseudo-photograph was sent to him without prior request made by him or on his behalf and that he did not keep it for an unreasonable time.

Possession offences

The following cases show how the courts have dealt with the possession of child pornography offences within the UK.

Christopher Sharp was the first person to be prosecuted in a case involving the Internet and he was fined £9,000 in October 1995 following Operation Starburst in the summer of 1995. Sharp admitted two charges of possessing indecent photographs of children under the age of 16 contrary to Section 160 of the Criminal Justice Act 1988.

In early 1996, Martin Crumpton, a former computer consultant, was sentenced to three months' imprisonment. Crumpton also admitted possession of indecent pictures of children and was the first person to be jailed in the UK for an offence concerning pornography and the Internet.

Graham Warren, 34, a statistician at Newcastle University, admitted ten specimen charges of possessing indecent photographs of children in November 1996. Warren was fined £1,000 and also ordered to pay £300 costs.

Dr George Reid, a research scientist in Glasgow, Scotland, was jailed for three months after being found guilty of possessing child pornography downloaded from a Japanese site on the Internet in October 1997.

Distribution offences

Distribution offences are more serious. There have been fewer court cases involving distributors of child pornography within England and Wales.

Arnold & Fellows (1997), the Birmingham University case, is perhaps the best-known. Arnold and Fellows faced a total of 18 charges under the Protection of Children Act 1978 and the Obscene Publications Act 1959. West Midlands Police Commercial Vice Squad swooped on the Department of Metallurgy at Birmingham University and discovered thousands of pictures stored in the computer system of youngsters engaged in obscene acts, following a referral from US Customs. Fellows had built up an extensive library of explicit pornography called 'The Archive', featuring children as young as three, on a computer at Birmingham University where he worked. The Archive could be accessed through the Internet across the world.

Fellows admitted four charges of possessing indecent photographs of children with a view to distributing them, and one of possessing obscene photographs of adults for publication. Arnold also admitted distributing indecent photographs of children. Fellows was jailed for three years, and Arnold for six months for providing Fellows with up to thirty pornographic pictures of children.

Simon Jackson, a computer consultant, was jailed for four months for sending indecent photographs of young children on the Internet in September 1996. Jackson admitted two counts of distributing indecent photographs or pseudo-photographs of children under the age of 16. He also admitted to one count of possession with intent to distribute indecent photographs of young children and one count of indecent assault on a child.

Father Adrian McLeish, 45, a Roman Catholic priest at St Joseph's Church in Gilesgate, Durham was sentenced for six years in November 1996. His activities were exposed during Operation Starburst. McLeish admitted 12 specimen charges of indecent assaults against two boys of 10, one aged 12 and another aged 18. He also admitted distributing indecent photographs, possessing them with intent to distribute them and being involved in the importation of pornographic videos of children.

Graham Fitchie, 37, of Merstham, Surrey had 10,751 pictures, 81 films and more than 500 pages of stories about child sex stored on computer hard disks and CD drives. Fitchie pleaded guilty to sending obscene images and films via the Internet, and to indecently assaulting the eleven-year-old boy in the original film. He was jailed for three years in July 1997.

The cases described here have involved offenders located within the UK. Given the global nature of the Internet, paedophile networks or disseminators of child pornography may be scattered around the world. The following discussion examines the problems faced by law enforcement bodies in such cases and assesses the effectiveness of new forms of self-regulatory schemes for fighting illegal content such as child pornography over the Internet.

Policing the Net

The global nature of the Internet and the development of the computer networks have presented law enforcement bodies with new and difficult challenges. How are the police to deal effectively with so-called cybercrimes, including the distribution of child pornography, when perpetrators may be located anywhere in the world? What has become clear in recent years though, following a number of high-profile police operations, is that co-operation between local police forces and co-operation between various national police forces all around the world has been effective in dealing with transnational criminal activity.

In July 1995, the police were involved in Operation Starburst, an international investigation of a paedophile ring which used the Internet to distribute graphic pictures of child pornography. Nine British men were arrested as a result of the operation, which involved other arrests in Europe, America, South Africa and the Far East. The operation identified 37 men worldwide.

There have been many similar police operations in relation to child pornography and the Internet, and the following table provides a list of these with short notes about the nature and the result of the operations.

Operation Name	Time	Place
Long Arm	1993	United States and Denmark
First Out	1994	Involved the Birmingham University prosecutions of Arnold and Fellows
Starburst	1995	Started in the UK and identified 37 suspects worldwide
Modem		Local operation by the Durham police involving the Father McLeish case
Innocent Images	1995	Ongoing FBI operation in the United States, which has generated 184 convictions by March 1998
Orchid Club Indictments	1996	16 people from the United States and abroad were indicted in San José, California for their participation in a child pornography ring called the Orchid Club, whose members used the Internet to share sexual pictures and conduct online chat during a child molestation session
Rip Cord	1997	The US Federal and New York state authorities have arrested more than 120 people suspected of sending child pornography over the Internet
Cathedral	1998	About 100 people in 12 countries were arrested

During Operation Cathedral, co-ordinated by the British police, more than 100,000 indecent images of children as young as two were recovered from one US-based paedophile club known as 'Wonderland'. According to the police, eleven people were arrested across the country. The paedophile ring was originally targeted by police in Sussex following a tip from the US customs service. Interpol also assisted the British police in the co-ordination of the operation. Seven men were charged in November 1998 with conspiracy to distribute indecent images of children in Hastings, East Sussex.

The involvement of British law enforcement bodies and police forces in such operations has undoubtedly helped them to develop their investigative techniques. However, there are several issues yet to be tackled by the law enforcement bodies if they are to be able to deal with cybercrimes effectively. Clearly, the main problem is the transnational nature of these crimes. Policing activity normally takes place within the borders of a nation state, and even at a national level traditional policing activity is localised. However, understanding computer technology and global communications networks such as the Internet poses another difficulty. National police forces within the UK are still learning about these issues at a time when resources and manpower remain limited.

Not all cybercrimes require high-tech policing, however. In a number of cases involving child pornography offences traditional policing methods proved effective. For example, it was an ordinary burglary that sparked the police investigation of Father McLeish after the thieves tipped the police off about McLeish's illegal activities. It was an informant, namely a paedophile serving a six-year jail sentence, who led police to another offender who appeared to be a respectable employee of a school publishing company in the Graham Fitchie case.

In an attempt to promote an understanding of the nature of policing the Internet, David Davis of the West Midlands police has produced *The Internet Detective – An Investigator's Guide* (Police Research Group, Home Office, 1998). This guide for police officers is an explanation of Internet policing issues and techniques. There are no plans at the moment by the Home Office to make the book more widely available, but a 'censored version' of the book can be obtained from the Home Office under the Open Code of Government Conduct process.

The creation of hotlines and self-regulatory solutions

In 1996 ISPs were coming under increasing pressure from a concerned public and the police to take action over child pornography available on the Internet. The initial warning to the ISPs providing services within the United Kingdom came from the ex-Science and Technology Minister Ian Taylor in August 1996. This followed the Metropolitan Police's attempt to ban around 130 Usenet discussion groups carried by the UK ISPs (a copy of the letter is at <http://www.cyber-rights.org/themet.htm>). Both Mr Taylor and the Metropolitan Police made it clear that the police would act against ISPs that provided users with pornographic and violent material. At that time the Internet content in question was mainly child pornography within Usenet discussion groups, but some of the groups identified by the Metropolitan Police did not involve any images at all.

This was the first time that the responsibility of ISPs for carrying illegal content within the UK was raised. Following the Metropolitan Police warning, self-regulation of the Internet industry rather than government regulation was seen as the best way forward by the government, the police and the Internet industry. This preference for self-regulatory solutions on the part of the UK government resulted in the establishment of the IWF in September 1996 (<http://www. internetwatch.org.uk>) and the Internet industry produced the 'Rating, Reporting, Responsibility

For Child Pornography & Illegal Material on the Internet'
proposals (<http://dtiinfo1.dti.gov.uk/safety-net/r3.htm>).
The Safety-Net proposal stated that the UK ISPs should be
responsible for their services and that they needed to
implement reasonable, practicable and proportionate
measures to hinder the use of the Internet for illegal
purposes, and to provide a response mechanism in cases
where illegal material or activity is identified.

> The IWF resembles a similar initiative in Holland which was
> endorsed by the first World Congress Against the Commercial
> Sexual Exploitation of Children in August 1996. The Dutch
> hotline Meldpunt (<http://www.meldpunt.org/>) was estab-
> lished by the Dutch Foundation for Internet Providers, Dutch
> Internet users, the National Criminal Intelligence Service and
> the National Bureau against Racial Discrimination with the
> involvement of a psychologist in June 1996.

The IWF is predominantly an industry-based
organisation supported by the UK government, the Home
Office, the Department for Trade and Industry and the UK
police. IWF launched its hotline for reporting illegal
material on the Internet in December 1996. It is fully
funded and supported by the UK Internet service
providers who oversee its operation. The IWF has an
e-mail, telephone and fax hotline so that users can report
materials related to child pornography and other obscene
materials. The IWF undertakes to inform all British ISPs
once they locate illegal content such as child
pornography. The ISPs concerned then have no excuse
in law that they are unaware of the offending material and
the UK police will be entitled to take action against any

'The government support the work of the IWF which was established . . . primarily in response to growing concern about child pornography on the Internet.'

Prime Minister Tony Blair, House of Commons, Hansard, Written Answers, 8 June 1998

See <http://www.parliament.uk>

ISP which does not remove the relevant content requested by the IWF.

The activities of the IWF in its first year mainly concentrated on the Usenet discussion groups. According to the IWF annual report published in March 1998, there have been 781 reports to the Foundation from online users and in 248 of them action was taken (206 involved child pornography, 16 adult pornography – see the IWF statistics at <http://www.internetwatch.org.uk/stats/stats.html> and the annual report at <http://www.internetwatch.org.uk/ press/annual.html>). These reports resulted in the review of 4,324 items, and the Foundation has taken action in 2,215 of them (2,183 referred to the police and 2,000 to ISPs). Some 1,394 of these originated in the US, while only 125 of the items originated in the UK. Despite the efforts of the UK organisation, only a handful of individuals have been charged with offences related to child pornography, and there are no reported cases so far.

The above figures tell us little as the actual amount of child pornography on the Internet is unknown. It is, therefore, difficult to judge how successful the UK hotline has been so far. Another downside is that the efforts of the organisation are concentrated on the newsgroups carried by the UK ISPs. This means that while illegal material is removed from the UK ISP servers, the same material will continue to be available on the Internet carried by foreign ISPs in their own servers. On the other hand, it is encouraging that only six per cent of the reported illegal material originates in the UK, and there are only a few criminal charges. This also suggests that the problems are located mainly elsewhere.

Overall, the expensive monitoring of the Internet at a national level is of limited value as the few problems created by the Internet remain global ones and thus require global solutions. While the availability and distribution of child pornography should undoubtedly be regulated, the main concern of enforcement authorities should, however, remain the prevention of child abuse – the involvement of children in the making of pornography, or its use to groom them to become involved in abusive acts. Hotlines are now widely developed within the European Union, but they remain only a partial solution and do not necessarily reduce the real-life problem of child abuse.

Conclusion

A new medium historically faces suspicion and is liable to excessive regulation as it sparks fears as to the potential detrimental effects it may have on society. Throughout history, governments have overreacted to all forms of communications technologies including the printing press, the telegraph, telephone, post, cinema, radio, television, satellite and video. Now, the Internet is receiving the same kind of treatment with various attempts to censor its content.

Books

Several books were censored and found to be obscene by governments and courts both in the UK and USA. See the Banned Books Online Project at <http://www.cs.cmu.edu/People/spok/banned-books.html>

Cinema

In 1912, the film industry created the British Board of Film Censors (BBFC) in order to bring a degree of uniformity to the standards of film censorship imposed by the many very disparate local authorities. It was set up in response to the Cinematograph Act 1909. In 1985 the BBFC became the British Board of Film Classification. BBFC also deals with videos and computer games. For a brief history of the BBFC see <http://www.bbfc.co.uk/>

Telephone

The Independent Committee for the Supervision of Standards of Telephone Information Services (ICSTIS) regulates the content and promotion of premium-rate telephone services. According to its code, services and promotional information must not contain material indicating violence, sadism or cruelty, or be of a repulsive or horrible nature, or involve the use of foul language. See ICSTIS at <http://www.icstis.org.uk/>

Radio

The Wireless Telegraphy (Content of Transmission) Regulations 1988 make it a specific offence to use obscene or grossly offensive language in transmissions. The police can directly follow up such offences, although the courts need evidence that the language used in the alleged offence is worse than that encountered in everyday life. The Radiocommunications Agency is the regulatory body and its web site is at <http://www.open.gov.uk/radiocom/rahome.htm>

Television

The Independent Television Commission (ITC) code exists to regulate broadcasting programmes. Section 1 of the ITC Code states that section 6(1)(a) of the Broadcasting Act 1990 requires that the ITC does all it can to ensure that every licensed service includes nothing in its programmes which offends against good taste or decency or is likely to encourage or incite to crime or lead to disorder or be offensive to public feeling. For example, in late 1998 the ITC decided that TV3 Denmark's screening of the film *Basic Instinct* was in breach of the code as the sexual content remained too lengthy and explicit for UK standards. ITC is at <http://www.itc.org.uk/>

The Broadcasting Standards Commission (BSC) is the statutory body for both standards and fairness in broadcasting. It is the only organisation within the regulatory framework of UK broadcasting to cover all television and radio. The BSC considers the portrayal of violence, sexual conduct and matters of taste and decency. A survey published in January 1999 by the BSC found that 'attitudes towards the portrayal of sexual activity on television have become more tolerant in the last six years'. See the BSC at <http://www.bsc.org.uk/>

Video

The Video Recordings Act 1984 gives power to the BBFC to classify videos for home viewing.

Satellite

The last satellite channel to be banned in 1998 is the Eurotica Rendez-Vous. From time to time the UK government continues to ban satellite channels with pornographic content. There have also been protests over the launch of Playboy TV, which promised 'Morgasms' in an advertising campaign in 1995.

Since the Internet became more widely available fears that it consists largely of pornography and other sexually explicit material which may be readily accessed by children have abounded. This guide has sought to dispel a number of the myths surrounding sex on the Net. Contrary to popular perceptions, Internet users are not bombarded with pornographic images the moment they log on to the Internet. Instead, pornography on the Internet has to be actively searched for in most instances, and in many cases paid for. In this sense, the Internet may be viewed as a less invasive medium than the television, for example, as pornography will seldom just appear on one's screen. Moreover, it represents only a tiny proportion of material that may be accessed through the Net. The moral panic about cyberporn has distracted attention away from the rich informational resources the Internet has to offer in our homes with the touch of a few buttons.

This guide has also examined how governments and law enforcement bodies are seeking to control pornographic material distributed and accessed over the Net. In the United States, attempts to introduce heavy-handed legislation, which would undoubtedly have had a chilling effect on the Internet, were struck down as unconstitutional. European countries, including the UK, have advocated instead the development of self-regulatory solutions, although there is a real danger that the use of filtering and rating systems, for example, may transform the Internet into a 'family-friendly' medium no more adventurous than the likes of the BBC. Furthermore, there is a potential danger that these tools will be used to filter legitimate discussion of sexually related matters such as homosexuality, AIDS and sexual abuse.

Moreover, the prime responsibility for ensuring an appropriate moral environment for children should not rest with the Internet industry. Instead, parents and teachers should be responsible for protecting children from accessing sexual or other material which may be harmful to their development.

It is the submission of this guide that any regulatory action intended to protect a certain group of people, such as children, should not take the form of an unconditional prohibition on using the Internet to distribute certain content which is freely available to adults in other media. The Internet should be treated no differently from any other medium, and the rights of adults should be respected.

There may be a case for commercial pornographers self-regulating themselves rather than relying on laws and regulations or technological solutions. There are already adult verification systems which require passwords and credit card numbers so as to exclude minors' access to such content on the World Wide Web. After all, pornography is a huge industry and is not interested in providing free porn to just anyone. For example, Adultcheck (<http://www.adultcheck.com>) is one of the main US-based companies regulating WWW pages carrying sexually explicit content on the Internet. Its system requires that both the willing adults and the providers are registered by paying fees to obtain usernames and passwords.

Child pornography is another matter. Its availability and distribution should be regulated, whether on the Internet or elsewhere. This guide has attempted to show that in the fight against child pornography on the Internet, law enforcement bodies all around the world have achieved some success. However, the main concern of enforcement authorities should remain the prevention of child abuse.

Calls for censorship of books, magazines, videos and satellite channels together with the debate on sex on the Net will undoubtedly continue into the new millennium, and we will continue to be 'depraved and corrupted' under the antiquated English obscenity laws. Keep an eye on <http://www.cyber-rights.org> for further developments! The author can be contacted at cyberporn@cyber-rights.org

Further Reading

Akdeniz, Yaman. 'Governance of Pornography and Child Pornography on the Global Internet: A Multi-Layered Approach' in L. Edwards and C. Waelde (eds.) *Law and the Internet: Regulating Cyberspace*, Oxford, Hart Publishing, 1997.

Avedon, Carol. *Nudes, Prudes and Attitudes*, Cheltenham, New Clarion Press, 1994.

Howitt, Dennis and Cumberbatch, Guy. *Pornography: Impacts and Influences*, London, HMSO, 1990.

MacKinnon, Catharine and Dworkin, Andrea. *In Harm's Way: The Pornography Civil Rights Hearings*, Cambridge, Mass., Harvard University Press, 1997.

O'Toole, Laurence. *Pornocopia: Porn, Sex, Technology and Desire*, London, Serpent's Tail, 1998.

Thompson, Bill. *Soft Core: Moral Crusades Against Pornography in Britain and America*, London, Cassell, 1994.

Walker, Clive and Akdeniz, Yaman (eds.). *Internet Law in the United Kingdom*, Harlow, Addison Wesley Longman (forthcoming).

Wallace, Jonathan and Mangan, Mark. *Sex, Laws, and Cyberspace: Freedom and Censorship on the Frontiers of the Online Revolution*, New York, Henry Holt & Company, 1996.